The Bodhrán Book

By Steáfán Hannigan

Ossian Publications

Acknowledgements

Written & Illustrated by Steáfán Hannigan

(except first two illustrations on page 8 and illustration on Page 14).
The Author and Publishers wish to thank the following individuals and institutions for their generous help and permissions to reprint copyright items
Paul Hottinger for front cover photo, Mark Vyvyan Jones for the brilliant cartoons, Mr.Saer and A.Lloyd Hughes at the Welsh Museum for photos and drawings of the Wecht, Norman Wilson for the pictures of the Corries, Jean Jenkins & Poul Rosving Olsen (World of Islam Festival Publishing Co.) for the photos in the history section, Mike Freeman for photos of Marc Moggy in chapter 24, Caoimhín O Danachair & Roinn Bhealoideas Eireann, Colaiste Na hOllscoile, Belfield, Dublin for the pictures of a boy playing the bodhrán, Mike Fleming & Patricia Moynihan for help with the tune transcriptions, Bill Bolger for the 'shaky bodhrán player' cartoon on p.19, Jak Kilby for his photos in the history section, Bord Failte The Irish Tourist Board for photos throughout the book. The Author and Publishers have tried their utmost to trace every single copyright item in this book, if inadvertently anyone's rights have been infringed upon, we apologize and beg to be informed.

The following are also available:

THE BODHRÁN BOOK PLUS DEMO CD (OMB8)
THE BODHRÁN BOOK DEMO CD, (OSSCD57)
THE BODHRÁN BOOK DVD (OSDV001)
THE BODHRÁN BOOK Only (OMB71)

Published by
Ossian Publications
14/15 Berners Street, London W1T 3LJ, UK

Exclusive Distributors:
Hal Leonard
7777 West Bluemound Road, Milwaukee, WI 53213
Email: info@halleonard.com

Hal Leonard Europe Limited
42 Wigmore Street, Marylebone, London WIU 2 RY
Email: info@halleonardeurope.com

Hal Leonard Australia Pty. Ltd.
4 Lentara Court, Cheltenham, Victoria 9132, Australia
Email: info@halleonard.com.au

www.wisemusicclassical.com

CONTENTS

		Page
1	About Bodhráns	7
2	The Beater	11
3	Getting Started	14
4	Skin Sounds	19
5	Reels 1	24
6	Jigs 1	28
7	Reels 2	30
8	Jigs 2	32
9	Triplets	34
10	Rim Playing	36
11	Reels 3	39
12	Jigs 3	42
13	Complex Reels	44
14	Complex Jigs	47
15	Other Styles	49
16	Hornpipes	54
17	Slip Jigs	55
18	Marches	58
19	Polkas	59
20	Slides, Waltzes, Mazurkas	60
21	Basics to remember	61
22	Care and Maintenance	62
23	Music Help	64
24	Bodhrán Manufacture	66
25	History	68
26	Discography	74
27	Music from Steáfán's tape 'Natural Selection'	77

"Beyond doubt it was the best bodhrán he had ever fashioned. It had a sonorous and most melodious tone and it carried farther than any instrument of its kind he had ever heard. It shivered and trembled when struck, its booming reverberations circulating around the kitchen long afterwards and diminishing delightfully until they were no more."
John B.Keane,"The Bodhrán Makers', Brandon Book Publishers, 1986, Dingle.

INTRODUCTION

Bodhrán playing is a musical skill as demanding as any other and yet even in the 1990s, it is still looked on as a second-rate instrument by the ignorant. In the right hands it is capable of providing a rich and varied accompaniment to traditional instruments, indeed, there is little to compare with the excitement generated by a duet for bodhrán and wooden flute.

The bodhrán has always had its detractors. Seamus Ennis, the respected musician and folklorist once remarked that the best way to play a bodhrán was with a penknife! The problem with the instrument lies partly in its low price (£40 - £100 in 1991) compared to that of other instruments, and partly in the ease with which a noise can be produced from it. Why some people go to an Irish session in a pub with a new bodhrán bought at a folk festival and then just bang away is beyond me. Surely they couldn't do this with their first guitar.

Fortunately, the climate of appreciation is changing. Great players like Damian Quinn, Tommy Hayes, Jim Sutherland, Maurice Griffen, Ringo McDonagh, and Gino Lupari, amongst others are giving the bodhrán its rightful place as a respected traditional instrument.

This book came from the workshops which I ran at Sidmouth and Whitby Folk Festivals over the past few years. Thanks to all who helped; especially to Fiona Larcombe, John Loesberg, Haydn Williams, David Ledsam, Paul Hottinger, Marc Vyvyan Jones, Marc Moggy, J.M.Hannigan, Bill 'Quark Examiner' Murphy,

Cormac Lankford, Dave Evans, Christine Sheard, Suzanna Lee, Chris Hamblin, Barry Nolan at Caroline Studios, Mike Flemming and Alan James for all their work and even more thanks to all who have been willing guinea pigs at my bodhrán classes. Thanks also to A.Lloyd Hughes and Mr.Saer at the Welsh Folk Museum, Jeremy Montague at the Bate Collection Oxford and Michael Kenny at the National Museum of Ireland for their help with the research.

If I could pass on any advice, I would suggest that you listen to the music long and hard, then go out and enjoy yourself. If you have any comments to make, please do drop me a line, c/o the publisher.

Good luck !

In principio erat bodhránum

1. ABOUT BODHRANS

A bodhrán is a frame drum, generally played with a double-ended beater or tipper. It is usually about 18 inches across (45 cms.) and 3-4 inches deep.(7.5-10 cms.) However, a bodhrán may be as small as a tambourine or as large as 36 inches across (90 cms.) and up to 6 inches deep(15 cms.). The wood used for the frame may be beech, ash or plywood and the drum will usually have one or two cross-braces which prevent warping and provide support for your hand. Some have a system for slackening or tightening the skin using a movable hoop inside the drum, these are adjusted with Allen screws.

Given the wide choice of drums available, there are basic things to look for when choosing a good bodhrán. The skin at normal room temperature (if possible, bodhráns should not be played outside) should be neither floppy to the touch nor pingy when struck. There should be no holes caused by the process of preparing the skin or by bites to the drum in a previous existence! Small differences in thickness are to be welcomed because they make different sounds when struck. If the skin is nailed on with upholstery tacks, make sure it isn't tearing away from them.

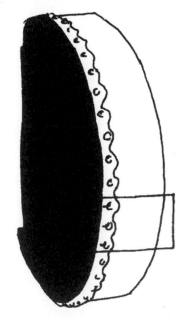
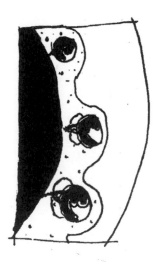

The skin may move a little but anything more than a couple of millimeters makes it slack and you would then have to re-skin the drum.

Bodhráns are usually made with calf, goat or deer skins, though there's nothing to stop you from using lama or camel skin. I have heard of drums made from greyhound and donkey skin. Each has its own peculiar charm. There are some drums made with plastic skins but these should be avoided at all costs. Animal skins vary in texture which means there is a difference in tone across the skin, producing many desirable effects. The same cannot be said for plastic.

The thickness of goat skin makes it by far the most suitable (and the most expensive). Calf skin drums are cheaper but more susceptible to changes in temperature and humidity. The standard of the best quality drums these days is superb, so be prepared to pay over £100 for a top quality instrument.

Many bodhráns from the best makers have a thicker area of skin running across the centre of the drum, corresponding to the spine of the animal. Skin from the soft underbelly of an animal is entirely unsuitable as this is too thin.

Spanish Frame Drum

N.American Frame Drum

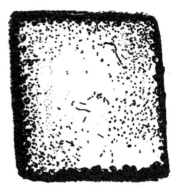
Duff from Morocco

The Rim

The rim is usually circular although it is also possible to make frame drums in other shapes. It is important that the rim is solidly constructed. Bodhrán rims can be made by glueing layers of wood together into a rim shape. If the bodhrán you're looking at has any of the layers coming apart it's best left alone! Both inner and outer edges should be rounded off and perfectly smooth, for the comfort of the player and to prevent undue wear on the skin. Any nails used in affixing the skin should not protrude on the inside of the rim as this is where your left hand will be later on and this could be dangerous. The rim should be finished with hard varnish, which prevents damage from both the beater and stray drinks, which are apt to be poured by intent (or accident) in the general direction of the unsuspecting bodhrán player.

The Cross-Piece

This is the final thing to look out for when buying a bodhrán. Much depends on your style. Some players still hold the cross-piece in the centre with their fingers curled round the bars. Others place the hand between the cross-piece and the skin and some players don't use one at all. Originally, the cross-piece was used to give strength to the frame but the better drums around no longer need one.

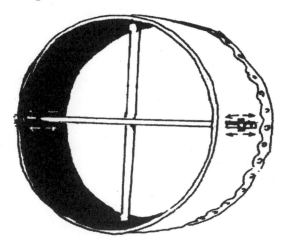

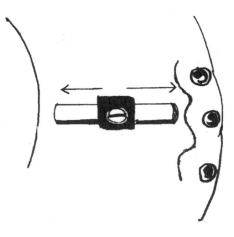

I prefer to have at least one cross-piece with which to lever the hand against the skin. Make sure that your hand fits neither too loosely nor too tightly between bar and skin - ideally, get an adjustable bar. Some makers have constructed a tuneable bodhrán where the tension of the skin can be regulated by means of a metal hoop, adjusted by screwthreads attached to the side of the rim.

Decoration

These days anything goes! The skin then can be decorated with beautiful Celtic figures and designs, either by the maker or by any good artist, using waterproof inks. Some makers decorate their rims with Celtic knot-work patterns.

I personally prefer a plain skin, unless the artwork is delicate and tasteful.

Beware! Decoration on the skin can hide all manner of faults, so check the skin quality for nicks, tears, small holes underneath the decorations. If the pattern covers the whole skin, the design will soon wear in the centre, so it may be better to go for an instrument with designs away from the centre of the skin or on the rim itself.

2. THE BEATER, Stick or Tipper

This causes more arguments than "Do you believe in leprechauns ? " Sticks come in all shapes and sizes and in many different woods.

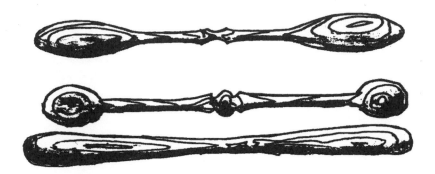

Most players have a selection of sticks for different occasions and effects. Try a few and settle on a couple (if you have never played bodhrán first look at the section on holding the stick). Please note that bodhrán tippers, like ballpoint pens are never there when you need them, so always carry a spare ! The sound of the drum can be changed by using an unusual stick - for example, you could try covering the ends with leather, this produces a dampened tone. Nylon brushes (from a drum shop) can be tied together so they face opposite each other, thus:

This makes a unique jazzy sound.

Different styles call for different sticks. In this book I will be teaching mainly the style of bodhrán playing where both ends of the stick are used in producing rhythms, this is sometimes called the double-end or double-stick style. For a double stick style it is usual to have a tipper about 9 inches long or the length of the

span from the thumb to the extended little finger. For single stick playing you need the equivalent of half a normal stick, with a leather loop on the end. You would usually hold this by slipping the index finger of your playing hand through the loop and putting the wooden end of the stick through the gap between thumb and forefinger, as in the diagram.

The hand can also be used in a variety of ways: instead of the stick, people use various combinations of fingers and thumbs to produce similar rhythms and below are some pictures of these different handstyles. For a fuller explanation please look up the section on handstyles.

between thumb and little finger, pivoting on the wrist

brushing the skin with the fingers slightly apart

One or two fingers extended and used as in the single stick method

Bodhráns come in all shapes and sizes !

3. GETTING STARTED

Hello there,

Use this book step by step. Read each section through before playing and you will be a bodhrán player in no time at all. Have patience. It would be a tremendous help if you were able to hum or whistle along to some traditional tunes first. If you don't have any idea about which records of traditional music to get, use the discography at the back of this book. You will notice that a few feature the bodhrán prominently. Those worth listening to for outstanding playing are listed with the track numbers in brackets.

It is worth repeating again that bodhrán playing is a musical skill as demanding as any other and yet even in the 1990s, it is still looked upon by the ignorant as a second-rate instrument. In the right hands it is capable of providing a rich and varied accompaniment to many a traditional instrument. Indeed, there is little to compare with the excitement generated by a duet between for example bodhrán and wooden flute.

Indian Frame Drum

If traditional music is completely new to you, try clapping along to the tape or record first. There is a chapter on the basics of musical notation for those of you who are not already familiar with it. I won't be using a great deal of it because it tends to frighten people but I think it really pays to know at least the basics.

However, back to the bodhrán. Before you start, sit up straight on your stool or a chair without armrests, relax your arms and shoulders and let your wrist do all the work. Try to make it really floppy, the action is a bit like shaking water of your hands. Most of the action takes place in the wrist and if you are too stiff, tension will build up in your arm, shoulder and neck. If this happens, you will soon get an ache which will affect your playing and you will be unable to play for long, so loosen up!

Your wrist should look
like this:

and not like this:

Preparing to play

In this section I am assuming that you have a bodhrán with two cross-pieces and that you are right-handed. If not, just adapt the instructions accordingly.

Hold the bodhrán in a vertical position by putting your left hand under one of the cross-pieces and resting it on the skin at the top of the drum. Your fingers should be held loosely together, not spread out.

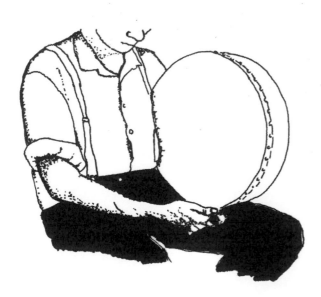

Next, place the drum under your armpit, resting it on your left thigh and hold it in place against your ribcage with your left forearm. You will not be able to get the whole drum under your arm, just 2 or 3 inches - that's all you really need.

Now pivot your left hand so that only the side of your thumb is touching the top part of the drum where the skin meets the rim. If you hit the centre of the skin with the other hand you should hear quite an open sound. Listen to the example on the tape.

Holding the stick

You hold the stick as you would hold a pencil, but with the 'point' turned towards your chest. Keep the stick held roughly in the middle so that it can pivot a little along its horizontal axis. If you remember to keep the stick parallel to the ground and parallel to the skin then there is little that can go wrong.

If you think of the bodhrán as a clock face, most of the action takes place between nine and six. (if you are left - handed, between three and six.) Later on, you will learn other techniques which go 'around the clock'.

When you want to strike the skin you use what would be the 'point' of the pencil, with the stick parallel to the ground and to the bodhrán. Don't worry about the other end of the stick - more about that later.

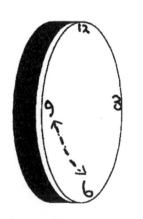

First of all, move the stick from nine o'clock to six o'clock, (three o'clock to six o'clock if you are left-handed) without touching the skin. At nine o'clock,(three o'clock) you should be able to see all your fingernails and part of your palm, and your stick should be horizontal (as in the first diagram).

16

At six o'clock, you should be able to see your thumbnail and a couple of knuckles and your stick should be vertical (as in the second diagram).

The stick is **never**, rocked back and forth with alternate ends hitting the skin. If you try to play in this way, you can have little control over what you are doing.

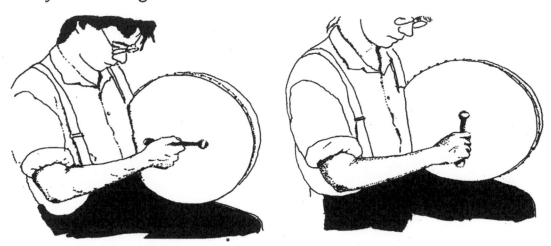

This time, making the same movement, try hitting the skin on the way down, remembering to use the part of the stick nearest to you. Hit the skin once between seven and eight o'clock and continue through to six. Now repeat with the stick in the vertical position, hitting upwards once between seven and eight o'clock and continuing through to nine. That was a downstroke followed by an upstroke.

In this book,
downstrokes are shown like this:

and upstrokes are shown like this:

The heavy arrows show that you should emphasise the beat by hitting the skin harder.

Dynamic Playing

I think that to get the best out of bodhrán playing, you must make the most of the dynamics of the instrument. This is why I have included the section on SKIN-SOUNDS (see chapter 4). Don't forget when you're learning you may be inclined to play too loudly, get used to adjusting the volume you play at, otherwise you'll be shunned like a musical pariah. Use all of the skin and the rim. Use your left hand to absorb the vibrations of the skin, thereby dulling the sound. This is called dampening the skin sound. To push it out, use your fingers, your thumb, the heel of your hand or a combination of all of them to push the skin out to get the maximum expression out of the instrument. Otherwise, you might as well play a paper bag. I can't stress this point enough - get to know your instrument.

4. SKIN-SOUNDS

There is an optimum tension for your bodhrán at room temperature. This is where the skin is not floppy to the touch, nor is it so tight that when you hit it you get a very high and bright, almost metallic, ping that lasts a fair while. The tone should be between the two, with a nice bass sound when struck in the centre of the drum. Listen to the taped example.

If the skin is a bit dull, restore it to life with indirect heat, for example by holding the bodhrán above a gas or electric stove. Don't hold it closer than 20 inches (50 cms) from the source of the heat or you will scorch the skin. You will learn in time just how long you have to keep it there. You can also tighten the skin by rubbing the heel of your hand along it or drying it with a hair drier - as one player put it; "Portable, economic but not very macho, unlike the small blowtorches I've seen used in pubs in England!"

If you find the skin is tight and pingy, apply water (certainly not beer or Guinness) to the inside surface of the skin. Use only a tiny drop of water at a time because if you use too much, the skin goes slack. Drop some into the middle of the skin, work it out towards the edges with the finger tips or a sponge and then throw away the excess. Some people use a house plant sprayer for this purpose. You will know in about five minutes whether it has done the trick. Listen to the taped example.

Most bodhrán players use water on the inside of the drum and dubbin, a grease preparation for softening and water-proofing walking-boot leather, on the outside - more about this in the CARE AND MAINTENANCE section (Chapter 22).

The bodhrán can be played in many different ways, with the hands and with the stick. There are three different categories of sound that can be made: OPEN , DEAD or FLAT, and PUSHED.

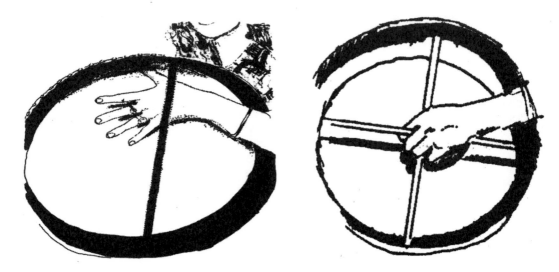

The **open** sound occurs when there is nothing preventing the skin from resonating. You can make this sound by placing the left hand at the top of the inside of the drum and resting the edge of the thumb at the point where the skin meets the wood of the rim (see diagram), or by holding the cross-piece and striking the drum in the centre of the skin. The sound will last for a couple of seconds. Listen to the taped example.

You should also look to see if the skin has any thick or thin patches or any scars or marks from fights in a previous life ! (Don't confuse these with the veins often found on calf skin). Marks or patches like this will produce a different sound when you hit them. Listen to the taped example.

You should also find that there is a distinctive and rather echoey sound around 3-5 cms from the rim edge. Listen to the taped example.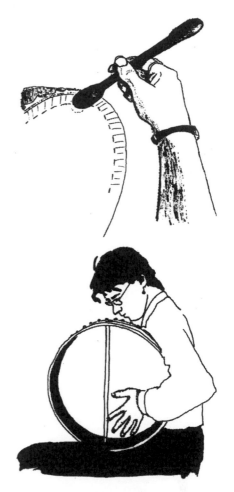

All these sounds can be used to great effect, so check them out before you start to play.

The **dead or flat** sounds occur when you put your hand on the inside of the skin and deaden the drum's natural ring. Try it for yourself. Put your hand, with your fingers out-stretched, at about twelve o'clock on the inside of the bodhrán and then hit the skin. Now move your hand to the centre of the drum and do the same thing. You should hear a short, dull thud in each case. Listen to the taped example.

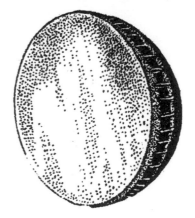

Later on when you are trying out rhythms, you will be able to vary the pitch and tone of the drum by putting your hand or fingers in different positions on the skin. Here is an example that you can try. Hold the bodhrán by the cross-piece, strike the drum and listen carefully to the sound. Now, using one finger, just touch the skin and strike it again, listening to the difference. Some drums will produce a note an octave higher just by doing this. Listen to the taped example.

The third main group of effects are the **pushed** sounds. These can be made by pushing out against the skin with the heel of your hand, by levering your fingers against the cross-piece or by pressing the skin out with the bodhrán held between your ribs and forearm. Listen to the taped example.

These positions can be uncomfortable if you are not used to them. If your bodhrán has a cross-piece, you must get your hand right underneath, so that your knuckles are touching it. Then brace your knuckles against the cross-piece while pushing the skin out with the heel of your hand. This is easiest in the middle of the drum. You should strike the skin near to the "bulge". The result is a high-pitched, tight ring. The sound will change according to where and how hard you press on the skin. Listen to the taped example. This uses the three different effects discussed above.

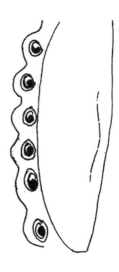

Open · · · · Flat · · · · Pushed

A Session

Killocrim Wren Boys, Co.Kerry

5. REELS - (1)

The reel, a Scottish invention according to some, is also the most basic Irish traditional rhythm, consisting of four beats per bar. For those of you uninitiated to the idea of beats, bars, etc., see chapter 23 (MUSIC HELP!). It is used all over the world and is the easiest to learn.

Watermelon

The word above provides the clue to the reel. It breaks up into four syllables:

Wa - ter - me - lon

The way we speak puts the emphasis on the first syllable. Thanks to the producers of 1940s Westerns, we often associate this beat with American Indians on the warpath!. Listen to the example on the tape.

To get the rhythm, you make four strokes on the drumskin: Listen to the example on the tape.

	Down	up	down	up
Count :	1	2	3	4

The large downward-pointing arrow denotes the most important and therefore the loudest beat. To get it, you hit the drum downwards with your stick.

Start with the stick horizontal and close to the skin of the drum, with the end closest to you at about nine o'clock. Now move the stick (downwards in an arc) towards a vertical position, pivoting it about your wrist and hitting the skin somewhere between seven and eight o'clock. In total, the stick should move through a quarter of a circle. This is called the downbeat. Look at the diagrams, they will help you. Listen to the example on the tape.

the start position (horizontal)

stick hits on the downbeat

stick at rest (vertical)

For the next beat, called the upbeat, you need to move the stick back from the vertical to the horizontal position using the same wrist - action. Move the stick upwards by pivoting the wrist, hitting the skin between seven and eight o'clock until the stick is horizontal again. Don't forget that throughout both the downbeat and the upbeat, it is the same end of the stick that hits the skin. Listen to the example on the tape.

stick at rest (vertical)

stick hits on the upbeat

the start position again

You have just learned the first two beats of the bar. The process is repeated for the next two beats. To make a good reel rhythm, you must emphasise the first beat in every four, as shown in the arrow-diagram. Try to keep your wrist loose and flexible as you practise this rhythm.

The symbols used in the diagram below are four arrows, followed by a repeat sign and a muliplied by four indication. You'll see these indications after every example. They tell you how many times the example is being played on the tape.

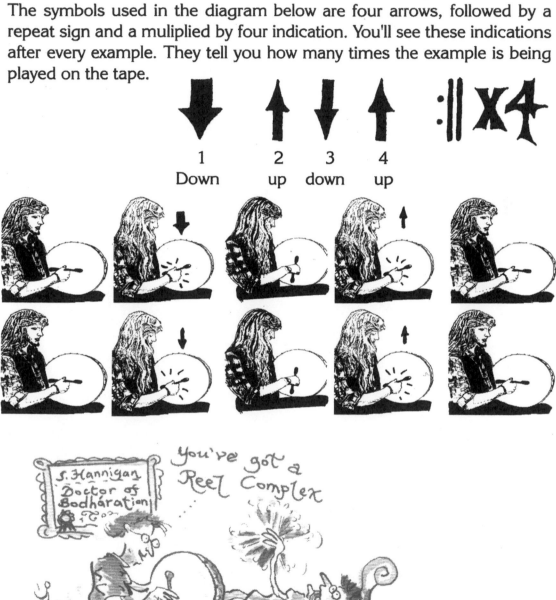

1	2	3	4
Down	up	down	up

6. JIGS (1)

According to Breandán Breathnach, one of the foremost authorities on Irish Music, the jig is the oldest surviving form of Irish dance music. For the novice bodhrán player it is a more complicated rhythm to master than the reel. Returning to food again, think of the following two fruits:

Pineapple Apricot

Putting the two words together gives us the jig rhythm, which consists of six beats to the bar, with a strong first and fourth beat. Split up, it looks like this (the counting is below):

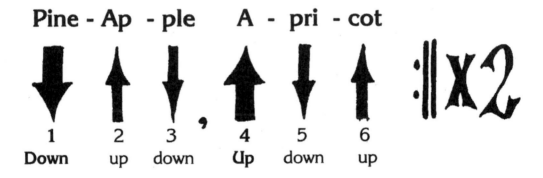

Pine - Ap - ple   A - pri - cot

1	2	3	4	5	6
Down	up	down	**Up**	down	up

The strong upbeat on the fourth beat of the bar is what most beginners fail to get correctly, so try the exercise shown in the arrow-diagram above until you feel confident. There are many different ways of playing the jig. Try the diagrams and see how they feel: Listen to the taped examples.

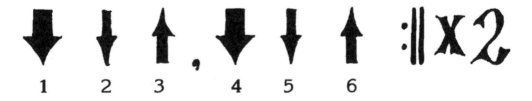

1   2   3   4   5   6

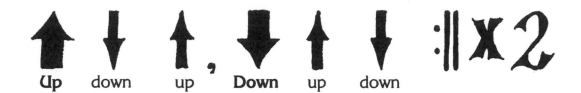

Up down up , **Down** up down :‖ x2

All the examples are played again on the tape at a faster speed.

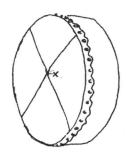

Do not go any further until you have mastered the ONE - two - three - FOUR - five- six rhythm of the jig. Get the upbeat on the FOUR perfect. If you are making a sliding sound on the skin, try to imagine hitting a spot about 2.5 centimetres or an inch below the surface. This will improve the sound.

7. REELS - (2)

Once you have mastered the basics of this rhythm, try the following pattern, not forgetting to start on a downbeat. At first, try counting out loud to yourself: Listen to the example on the tape.

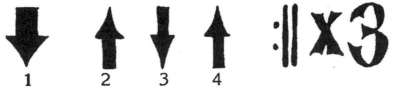

This places the emphasis on the first beat of the bar.

Another rhythm common to Irish reels involves emphasising the third beat of the bar instead. Try this, again starting on a downbeat. Listen to the example on the tape.

This gives the music a great lift. A good player can move in and out of both patterns effortlessly. You can practise this by trying the following pattern. Listen to the example on the tape.

You could also experiment by hitting the skin close to the rim on the beat you want to emphasise and returning to the centre of the drum for the other beats, as shown in the diagram. Listen to the example on the tape.

The right hand holding the bodhrán stick would move across the skin for these strokes, hitting the skin at the places marked by an X in the diagram.

You can also introduce a skip into the reel by trying out the following exercises: once you get the first one correct move on to the next, building up speed as you go.

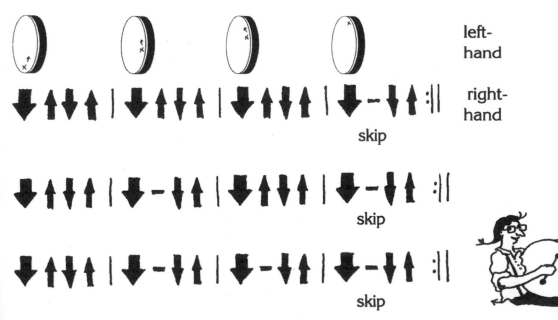

31

8. JIGS - 2

You can get many variations on the jig by altering the direction of the stick and by leaving gaps where you do not hit the skin at all. For some of the examples below you have to move your hand quickly in order to play two strokes in the same direction without losing time. It's tricky but it will come with practice. Try the following and listen to the example on the tape.

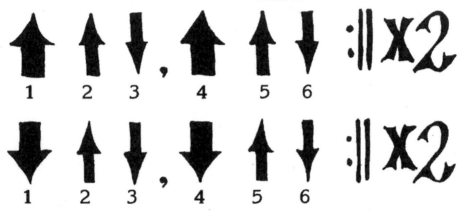

Now try skipping a beat. This helps jig rhythms to bounce along:

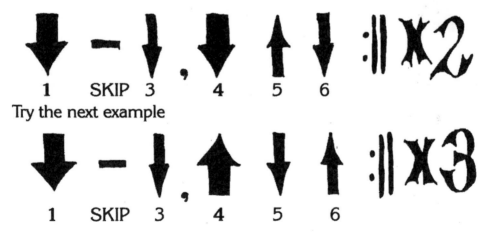

Try the next example

Emphasise the first and fourth beat of each group of six. Try the following examples.

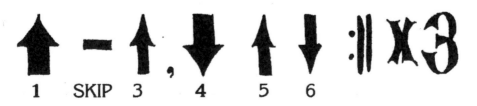

Next example:

If you find it difficult to put the skips into the jig try the following examples:

Fleadh Nua, Ennis, Co.Clare

33

9. TRIPLETS

With practice, these are easy. If you have been practising the reel section, you may have found the stick sometimes hitting the skin at both ends. This is the triplet that we are after.

Start by playing a reel, holding the stick loosely in your hand. On the first downstroke bring the stick towards the vertical position, rotating your wrist and trying to make your knuckles parallel with the ground.

This will incline the far end of the stick towards the skin, hitting it on the way down. Follow this with an upbeat and you have the triplet. The sequence is down - tap - up, down - tap - up this is shown by the inclusion of a " **T** " in the diagrams.

As a beginner, you will find that this extra beat sometimes occurs by accident but you should learn to control it. You will find the triplet easier at moderate speeds; it's not easy to play it slowly.

The triplet should not interfere with the regular beat and the wrist action should still be down - up, down - up . If you do find it difficult, hold the stick closer to the skin and try again. Try the following exercise and listen to it on the tape:

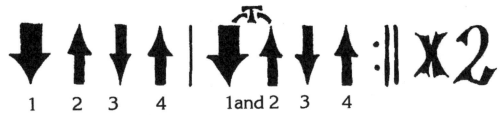

Both sections should take the same time.

It is possible to use triplets on the upbeats but this is rarely done because you have to twist your wrist at an uncomfortable angle in order to get the effect. You do the upstroke, rotating your wrist until your knuckles are parallel with the surface of the drumskin, which brings the stick into contact with the skin. You then follow on with the downstroke, look at the diagram below. Try that. Listen to the example on the tape.

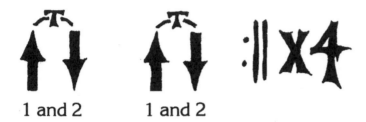

Remember that it is always better to have too few than too many triplets! Try this in jig rhythm.

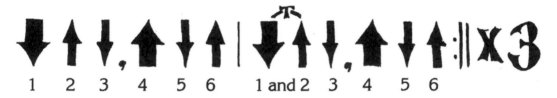

Triples

10. RIM-PLAYING.

In order to get the clickety-clack sound that's either loved or hated by so many, you must play on the frame or rim itself. This stroke is also known as a rim shot. Keep the stick in the same position that you would use if you were playing the skin and move the bodhrán. Turn it through

ninety degrees, so that the part of the drum underneath your armpit is brought across the front of your body, as shown .

Now imagine a line running down the centre of the rim. Put your stick parallel to the side of the rim and try to keep your thumb pivoting along this imaginary line. The edge of the beater hits the edge of the rim as in the diagram.

Try the exercise pictured below, moving the stick from horizontal to vertical and back again. Listen to the taped example:

You should be able to do triplets in the same way that you would on the skin. Listen to the taped example. In the diagram below the —T— sign represents the top of the stick hitting the skin.

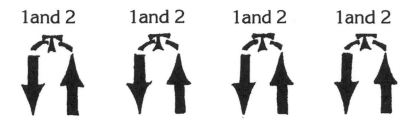

Some people also run the edge of the stick along the nails which hold the skin in place, to get a washboard effect. Listen to the taped example:

Once you are confident about playing rim-shots, try combining them with hitting the skin as in the taped example. Listen to the taped example:

Some people play on the rim for eight bars of the tune and then go back to the skin for the rest. Others combine both in rapid succession. Try also what is called the single-ended style of playing (for more details about this, see the section on OTHER STYLES, see chapter 15), where the working end of the stick moves up and down along the imaginary line shown in the earlier diagram.

A Bodhrán Maker, Co.Kerry

11. REELS - (3)

When you can move easily between the two rhythmic patterns in REELS-(2) you could try one of the following cross-rhythms, where the beat illustrated goes across the expected reel rhythm. Go slowly at first, you will soon get the hang of them with practice. Listen to the examples on the tape before you start. These can be played as variations during a tune but do be careful as many people could be put off if you play them in a session as they alter the rhythm unexpectedly. Try them among consenting adults first!

Start on a downbeat and play all the strokes shown, then try leaving out all the white arrows. Listen to the example on tape.

1 2 3 4   1 2   3 4 1 2 3 4   1 2 3 4

The rhythm becomes apparent when you practise it! (This rhythm depends upon the four groups of four beats being taken as a whole unit.)

Another one you could try is the following:
Listen to the example on tape.

1   2   3   4   1   2   3   4

39

This is more difficult because you have to hit the drum twice on a downstroke. To do this you start by placing the first downstroke higher up on the bodhrán than usual, as shown in the diagram.

The strokes do not conform to the usual pattern of DOWN UP DOWN UP given in the earlier examples.

Another way of making the music more interesting is to skip beats and create a more open sound. Diagrams for this kind of rhythm can be quite difficult, as it is easier to listen to the beats than to read them off a page. Listen to the example on the tape and follow the diagram below a couple of times before trying to play it. In the diagram, the — means that you should move your hand as if to play, without actually hitting the skin. Listen to the example on tape.

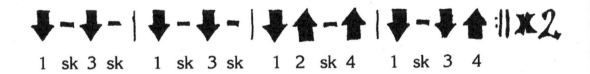

| 1 | sk | 3 | sk | 1 | sk | 3 | sk | 1 | 2 | sk | 4 | 1 | sk | 3 | 4 |

Or you could try this one: (add it to the above)

Other ways to make your rhythms more complicated involve using the techniques described in the sections on TRIPLETS (chapter 9) and SKIN - SOUNDS (Chapter 4).

You could take the second example above and move your left hand across the skin, altering the tension to go from the pushed to the open skin-sound in the first four bars, as in the taped example. Listen to the example on tape.

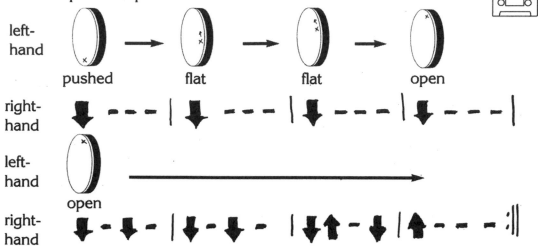

You could perhaps replace the first four bars with the following example, while changing the pitch of the drum as before by moving your left hand across the skin of the bodhrán. Listen to the example on tape.

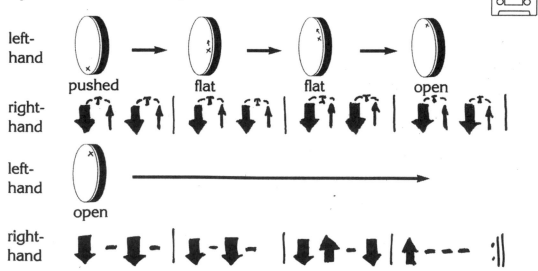

These patterns can be put into any reel and the possibilities are endless. Why not make up some of your own? Experiment with hitting different parts of the skin and the rim (for help with this, see the section on RIM-SHOTS, chapter 10).

12. JIGS - (3)

When you play the next example, move your stick past the edge of the bodhrán after hitting the skin on the third beat. This time, bring it up hitting the rim for the fourth beat. Play the fifth and sixth beats on the skin as usual. This introduces a click into the rhythm which is quite effective in jig playing. (The click is shown by a " C " in the middle of an arrow). This is sometimes known as a rim shot. Listen to the example on tape.

You can put the click in anywhere! To introduce it on the first beat, you hit the part of the rim nearest to you on the downbeat. Listen to the example on tape.

Again, there are many variations on this.

Try this. Listen to the example on tape.

And try this. Listen to the example on tape.

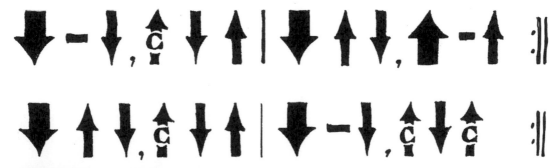

Once you have sorted out the examples above, you can make up your own. Things get more complicated when you introduce TRIPLETS (Chapter 9) so have a good look at that section before going any further. Also, read the section on SKIN-SOUNDS.(Chapter 4)

Here are two more rhythms which are on the tape. Listen to the examples.

13. COMPLEX REELS

Before you start this section you should be happy about using all the techniques that appeared earlier in the book. We start by putting in rim-shots.

To get this effect in the reel-rhythm, hit the edge of the drum close to the tacks, on the first (or third) downstroke of each group of four. You may have to move the bodhrán away from you and support it with your left hand whilst hitting the rim.

The trick is to hit the rim and carry on with the stroke, turning the wrist for the second stroke in the usual way. Try this yourself. Listen to the example on the tape.

For the first four bars and the last bar there is a click on the first beat of the bar. Don't forget to get into the proper position by moving your stick up past the rim on the previous beat. In bars five and six, the click occurs in the third beat of the bar. When written down as an arrow-diagram it looks like this, the click is represented by the ' C ' sign:

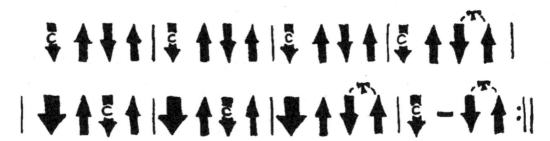

When you add the triplets the fun starts! (Chapter 12 for the inexperienced) You can create patterns which look like the example below. Listen to the example on the tape.

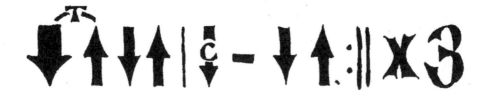

To help you brush up on triplets, try the following exercises. Listen to the two examples on the tape.

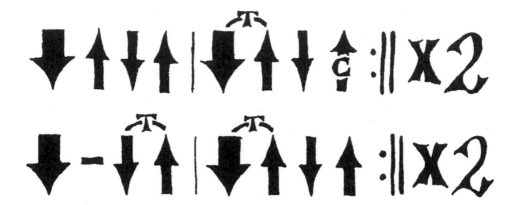

You can combine these with the skin-sound variations to produce a great rhythm like the next one. Listen to the example on the tape.

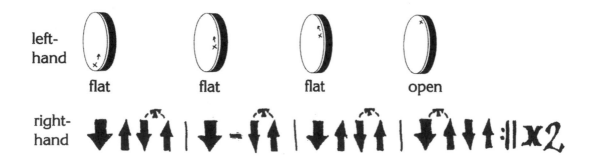

left-hand   flat   flat   flat   open

right-hand

As you can see from the diagram above, your left hand moves from the first position to the fourth and is ready at the end of the series (position 5) to do the whole thing over again.

Now that you're more confident in your playing, try the following exercises:

As a start you could try the following exercises to get you used to using both parts of the drum. Keep repeating the exercises until they can be done effortlessly. The trick is to be ready to hit the rim on the third beat. Start slowly at first and build up speed gradually. There are no examples of these rhythms on the tape.

The first version:

$$\Downarrow - \updownarrow \Uparrow \mid \Downarrow - \updownarrow \Uparrow \mid \Downarrow - \updownarrow \Uparrow \mid \Downarrow - \Updownarrow \Uparrow \| \times 3$$

Once you are confident with this, try the second version as follows:

$$\Downarrow \Uparrow \updownarrow \Uparrow \mid \Downarrow \Uparrow \updownarrow \Uparrow \mid \Downarrow \Uparrow \updownarrow \Uparrow \mid \Downarrow - \Updownarrow \Uparrow \| \times 3$$

This incorporates the rim and the skin and you have to make sure that you get your hand up in time to produce the 'click' sound. Now try out your own ideas.

Girls celebrating the birthday of the Prophet, singing to the accompaniment of the bendir. Ouzad, Morocco.

14. COMPLEX JIGS

Once you feel confident with jig rhythms you will want to introduce more variety into your playing. I trust that you have looked at the sections on TRIPLETS (Chapter 9) and SKIN-SOUNDS (Chapter 4), so here goes!

Try to incorporate the top end of the stick in your playing, as shown in the following examples. Listen to the examples on the tape.

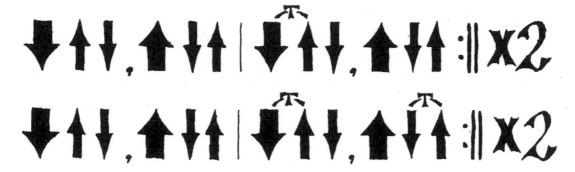

Try all the variations above until you can put a triplet in with confidence. Practise incorporating the various skin-sounds by trying the following example. Listen to the example on the tape.

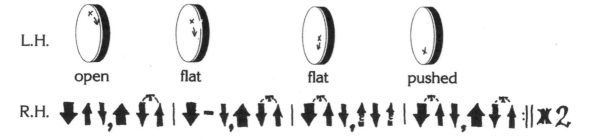

Remember that this is just one of many possible rhythms.

Like reels, jigs can be played using syncopated (off-the-beat, jazzy) rhythms. Try the next one. Listen to the example on the tape.

1 sk 3 sk 5 sk

A good player will incorporate some or all of the examples above during the course of an evening's performance. Most players will use these techniques either to follow the tune as closely as possible or to provide an interesting cross-rhythm that will contrast with the music. Don't forget to include rim shots in your jig playing! Listen to the examples on the tape.

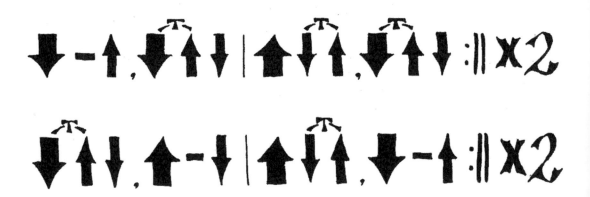

15. OTHER STYLES - ONE END OR TWO ?

Most bodhrán players use both ends of the stick but there are some who produce terrific rhythms with either one end of a long stick or with a short stick that has a leather thong attached.

To achieve the triplet sound with one end of the stick move your wrist twice as fast as you normally would, hitting the drum with the same end three times in succession. This produces the same sound, except that with a two-ended triplet the stick strikes different parts of the skin, creating a difference in tone. Listen to the two examples on the tape. The first example uses a double stick style the second uses this single stick style.

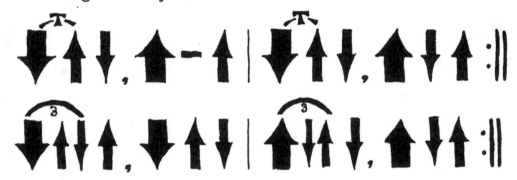

The sign ⌢3 tells you to play the group of three in the same time as a group of two. A further point to note is that there is more energy involved in one-ended playing and this affects the sound produced.

The two-ended stick can be held as in the diagram on the left or with one end resting in the palm of the hand.
Try both ways. Listen to the example on the tape.

You can also play a triplet by holding the stick in such a way that it rebounds off the skin of the bodhran. With practice you will be able to control the number of bounces. Listen to the example on the tape, the sign ||||ıı represents the stick bouncing on the skin for two beats.

The best part of the drum-skin for trying this technique is the area closest to the rim. Hold the stick loosely and try to bounce it down from the horizontal and up from the vertical position, almost as if you were using it as a paintbrush. This technique depends upon the tension of the skin but it usually works. The main drawback is that it is a very quiet sound.

Hearing someone play with a stick and thong is an amazing experience. (Today there are few players of this style. Musicians such as Val Knight from Somerset continue this tradition which incorporates a high degree of syncopation playing from the rim to the skin with great ease. The best player in this style in Great Britain was the great John Claydon who played for the Irish Dance team Clan na Gael.)

John Claydon

The thong is attached to the index or middle finger, with the knob appearing between thumb and index finger, the hand closing loosely around it. The working end of the stick moves from eight o'clock to two o'clock and the hand moves across this arc, rather than up and down as in the double-ended style.

playing 2-ended

Other styles - Hands

Some people (notably the singer Christy Moore) use their hands rather than a stick to play the bodhrán. In France, Carlo Rizzi who is the percussionist with 'La Grande Bande Des Cornemuses' uses a tambourine to brilliant effect, producing an amazing array of rhythms and sounds. Hand styles vary from using the back of the index and middle fingers like a one-ended stick to using the thumb and the little finger in opposition.

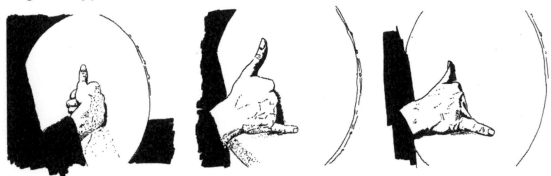

This can be quite effective when the bodhrán has a low boom and is amplified through a microphone. Listen to the example on the tape.

The hand style of playing also provides sounds that cannot be made with a stick. A thumb roll, where friction between thumb and bodhrán causes the thumb to skid along the surface sounds great if the bodhrán has jingles (often metal discs or bottle-tops, which rattle when you play the drum). Listen to the example on the tape.

Hitting the skin with the edge of the thumb in the same way as a slap-funk bass player, can also produce an interesting sound. Sometimes a player will flick his or her fingers outwards from the palm of the hand while using the other hand to vary the pitch of the skin as in a stick style. Listen to the example on the tape.

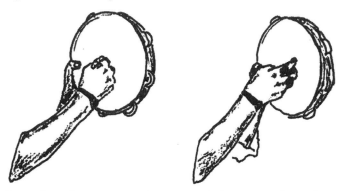

Most of these hand styles are unique to the particular players such as Christy Moore and John Skelton (from The House Band) for example, so search them out and find out how they do it. Hand styles are really underestimated amongst younger players!

16. HORNPIPES

The Hornpipe is of English origin, it assumed its present form at the latter end of the 18th century when it changed over from triple time (3/2) to common time (4/4).

These dances have a bouncier rhythm than reels, with a well-defined accent on the first and third beat. Play them in the same style as reels but hold on longer to the first and third beats and shorten the second and fourth beats, as in the words:

HOL - LY   I - VY

1   2   3   4

Listen to the example on the tape.

Use triplets where the tune has triplets and keep the playing firmly on the first and third beats of the bar. Otherwise, the same rules apply as for reels. Listen to the example on the tape.

17. SLIP JIGS

Petrie, a collector of Irish Music in the 18th century suggests that the slip jig or hop jig evolved from a genre of ancient Irish vocal melodies but there's no doubt that these were also common in England.

Slip jigs are similar to jigs, with an extra three beats to every bar. The rhythm can be heard as three groups of three. You could use the words Apple tree, Orange tree, Lemon tree to help you remember the rhythm.

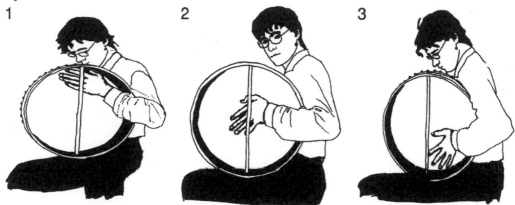

While playing the beats shown in the diagram below, try to move your hand down the skin throughout the nine beats of the rhythm. Fig 1 shows the position for the first three beats, Fig 2 for the next three beats and Fig 3 for the last three. You could then reverse the direction for the next series of nine or return straight to the top, ready to start again as in the first figure. This hand movement will produce differing skin tones as you play. The commas between the arrows are there to ensure that you devide the bar up into three groups of three. Listen to the example on the tape.

And the other way. Listen to the example on the tape.

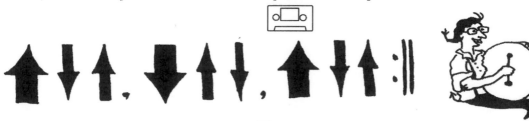

This is the most basic rhythm for the slip jig and can soon get repetitive. Try the following rhythms as well. Don't forget that a — indicates that you should skip a beat but move your hand as if playing. Where the ninth beat is a downbeat you must either quickly prepare for another or reverse the series.

Try this example:

The skip can be placed anywhere in the three sections and you can put in as many as you like to vary the play. Listen to the example on the tape.

And the next one. Listen to the example on the tape.

The third one. Listen to the example on the tape.

Once you have mastered the skip, try putting in the triplet. If you have forgotten how to do it, check the relevant section.(Chapter 9). Listen to the example on the tape.

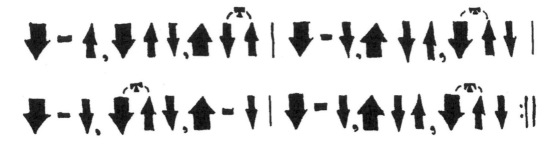

Now try this one. Listen to the example on the tape.

You must make sure that when you play the triplet it takes up **NO EXTRA TIME** , otherwise you are heading for big trouble ! You must play 1 skip 3 and 1 and 2 3 in the same time as 1 2 3.

The Slip Jig

Now try these exercises again, incorporating the left hand movements described at the beginning of the chapter. Once you are comfortable with all these patterns, you will be able to add variety to your slip jigs - but don't feel that you have to do everything at once. The most important thing is to emphasise the primary beat in each group of three:

1 2 3 **4** 5 6 **7** 8 9

The last example is played again whilst pushing out the drum skin. Listen to the example on the tape.

18. MARCHES

The march is probably the oldest form of music handed down to us from times past. The Irish were frequently to be found on the continent in the 12th to 15th centuries working as mercenaries and marches were an important part of a soldier's life. There are still clan marches from that time being played today.

These can be in three-time or four-time. When playing them, pick out the main beats. Triplets are again a good way of bringing out the rhythm. Try to follow the shape of the tune. If it has clearly defined stops then you should reflect that in your playing. Think also of the way a military side-drummer would play a march.

Perhaps you could use this rhythm (in 4/4 time). Listen to the example on the tape.

Whatever you do, try to keep it crisp and unfussy.

19. POLKAS

Some people suggest that the polka came originally from Poland hence the name. Polkas are generally played in a way which follows the shape of the tune (This means that where the tune has triplets in the melody or has rests you should attempt the same). Sometimes this may be at double the speed of the tune. What is important is to emphasise the strong beats and to make the accompaniment interesting with changes in dynamics and rhythm, giving the tune a lift. The polka is a dance in two-time so it's more akin to the reel than to the jig. Listen to the polkas on the tape and join in, remembering that this is a light and fast dance (This is a literal transcription of the rhythm). Listen to the example on the tape.

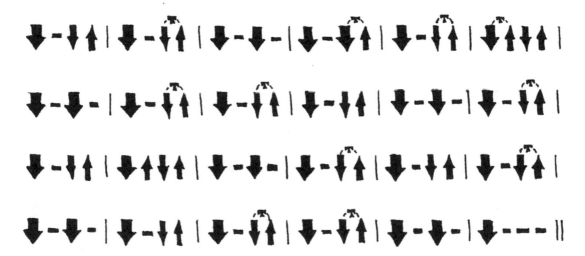

This can be seen as variations on a theme shown below:

You could also emphasise the off-beat by playing as below. Listen to the example on the tape. Look at the difference between the two:

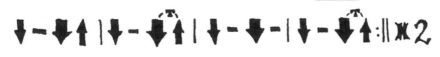

20. SLIDES, WALTZES and MAZURKAS

Slides are aften used in set-dancing, and are similar to jigs in having groupings of three quavers - but in slides, there are four groups of three per bar. The emphasis is usually on the first beat of each three, as shown in the arrow-diagram below. Listen to the example on the tape.

WALTZES

Well-known in the Ballroom Dancing circles, the waltz is in 3/4 time. These are popular in some ceilidh bands. You play them with a slow, deliberate first beat. Listen to the example on the tape.

MAZURKAS

These 3/4 dances are still popular in parts of Ireland such as Donegal and are often played in sessions to break up the jigs and reels. The catch is in the last bar of every eight bar section, which has a peculiar rhythm involving stops in the music. Listen to the taped example and follow the arrow-diagram. Listen to the example on the tape.

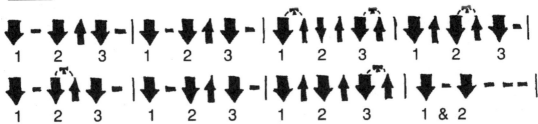

21. BASICS TO REMEMBER

Check that the skin is not too tight or slack before playing,

Place the bodhrán under your armpit, resting on your thigh. It is held in place by the upper forearm pressing the rim against your ribs.

Hold the stick firmly (but not stiffly) towards the middle, between thumb and finger. Hold it like a pencil but turn the "point" in towards your chest.

Keep the stick parallel to the ground and to the skin. Initially you should only use the end of the stick nearest to you.

Nearly all rhythms start with a strike downwards.

You hit the bodhrán on the downstroke by travelling from nine o'clock to six o'clock,(three o'clock to six o'clock for left-handers) hitting the skin between seven and eight o'clock (four and five) and following the movement through to six. You do the reverse for the upstroke.

To play a triplet, your knuckles should be in a horizontal plane as you do the downstroke.

Always listen to the tune before joining in. Music snobs (or the great unwashed,as my Cork friend says.) do not consider bodhrán players to be real musicians, so prove them wrong. Pick up the beat first and try to follow the tune. Keep the beat simple until you know what you are doing.

Use your other hand to make the three kinds of skin-sound - **OPEN** , **FLAT** and **PUSHED** . Remember that the centre and the edge of the skin also provide different tones. This is the key to good playing

Remember ; there is no need to play loud all the time. Good dynamics = good playing !

Good luck !

22. CARE AND MAINTENANCE

If you look after your bodhrán it will last a lifetime, although you may have to get the skin changed every ten years or so.

The basic rules are easy to follow. Keep the bodhrán in a warm, moderately dry atmosphere when not in use. Do not hang it above your fireplace, nor leave it in your cellar. Somewhere where you yourself would like to sit would do nicely.

If you travel with your bodhrán, please put it in a decent case and not a plastic bag. Preferably, get a wooden case made. Never leave it locked up in a car on a hot day or on a sunny window sill, or the skin will rip apart with one heck of a bang !

If your drum gets too tight and pingy, put some water on the inside of the skin. Use only a little and rub it well in. To keep the skin in good order, use a small amount of preservative like dubbin (on the OUTSIDE of the skin only) every six months or so. This keeps it lasting longer. Please note that the place for beer is in your stomach and NOT in your bodhrán.

Check that the skin is not pulling away from the nails and give the rim a lick of paint or varnish if necessary. If the rim is made from a laminate check from time to time that it is not coming apart..If this is the case take the bodhrán to a reputable instrument repairer.

That's all there is to it!

23. MUSIC - HELP!

Is this what you think of written music?

This is the help section for non-musicians. Music is written down in note form, the same way as you would take down notes in a school lesson. It is just there to assist you, so don't be afraid of it ! It is useful to be able to understand a bit, to help you work out rhythms and learn how to play in time.

These are the lines of the stave. Most music is divided up into equal measures called bars. The vertical lines are called bar-lines and they separate the measures.

At the start of a piece of music is usually written the time-signature, these are the numbers shown in the diagram. They tell you not the speed of the tune but how many beats there are in the bar and what kind they are. In 3/4 time, the top number tells you that there are three beats per bar and the bottom one tells you what kind of beat it is and how long it lasts: 4 = a quarter note or crotchet.

Remember this:

3   TOP NO.   eg 3 = HOW MANY
4   BOTTOM NO. eg 4 = WHAT KIND

:‖ This symbol is a repeat sign. You repeat the examples to the left of the symbol.

Here follows a summary of the different time-signatures you are likely to meet and what they mean.

Key Signature	Music Pulse	Played	Beats per bar	Type of beat	Uses
2/4	♩ ♩	↓1 ↑2 OR / ↓1 −+ ↑2 ↓+	**2**	Crotchet (or quarter note)	**POLKAS MARCHES**
4/4 OR **C**	♩ ♩ ♩ ♩ OR ♩. ♫ ♩. ♪ [Hornpipes]	↓1 ↑2 ↓3 ↑4 OR / ↓1 ↑2 ↓3 ↑4	**4**	Crotchet (or quarter note)	**MARCHES REELS HORNPIPES SET DANCES**
3/4	♩ ♩ ♩	↓1 ↑2 ↓3 OR / ↓1 −+ ↓2 ↑+ ↓3 ↑+	**3**	Crotchet (or quarter note)	**WALTZES SOME MARCHES**
6/8	♫♪ ♫♪	↓1 ↑2 ↓3 ↑4 ↓5 ↑6	**6** (2 groups of three)	Quaver (or eighth note)	**JIGS MAZURKAS**
9/8	♫♪ ♫♪ ♫♪	↓1 −2 ↓3 ↑4 ↓5 ↑6 ↓7 ↑8 ↓9	**9** (3 groups of three)	Quaver (or eighth note)	**SLIP JIGS SET DANCES**
12/8	♫♪ ♫♪ ♫♪ ♫♪ OR ♩♪ ♩♪ ♩♪ ♩♪	↓1 −2 ↑3 ↓4 −5 ↑6 / ↓7 −8 ↑9 ↓10 −11 ↑12	**12** (4 groups of three)	Quaver (or eighth note)	**SLIDES**

Note Values

Name		Count
Whole note or Semibreve	𝅝	4 beats
Half note or Minim	𝅗𝅥	2 beats
Quarter note or Crotchet	♩	1 beat
Eighth note or Quaver	♪	1/2 beat
Sixteenth note or Semiquaver	𝅘𝅥𝅯	1/4 beat

Note Pyramid

The total value of each row is equal to the semibreve on top.

24. BODHRAN MANUFACTURE

This chapter is not a guide to making your own Bodhrán. It is a short article which gives you a brief guide as to how most professional makers would construct an instrument.

At present there are about 20 professional or semi-professional bodhrán makers in Ireland and the U.K., many will be glad to talk to you about the way they make a drum. Some will also be happy to make an instrument to your specifications. The relationship between a good maker and player is important. The person who makes my drums will make changes to the design to suit the way I play.

Beech, Ash or laminates are used to make the frame, which is usually about 8-14 mm thick. The frame is constructed around a mould made from M.D.F. or chipboard or similar material. If the wood for the frame is not flexible enough it is shaped around a bending iron. This prevents the wood from splintering as it is clamped around the mould.

The wood is offered up to the mould and measured so that the frame is the correct circumference.

The wood is then planed down to the surface of the mould to give the correct depth.

Next the wood is measured and cut so that the edges of the rim to be joined together fit perfectly. If the bodhrán is constructed of a laminate then successive layers are glued and clamped together with their edges in a different place for strength. If only one thickness is used then the edges are joined by a scarf joint where the two edges are feathered and glued.

An internal hoop or inner support rim is added which gives strength to the frame and provides a strong area into which tacks or staples can be put. At this stage any tuning mechanisms are added. The rim is then filed and sanded smooth prior to painting or varnishing.

One or more cross pieces are added if required and then the skin is tacked or stapled on wet and then allowed to dry before being tested.

The sticks or tippers are turned separately on a lathe. Usually the bodhrán maker would make the stick as well.

The finished article

25. HISTORY OF THE BODHRAN

There is a great deal of discussion among bodhránophiles as to the origin of the instrument. This piece is but a brief synopsis; more scholarly people than I have written, in great detail, on the subject.

Most people would agree, there are two main theories: the first suggests that it was the development of a domestic sieve or winnow, whilst the second theory proposes that it arrived in Ireland via contact with other cultures.

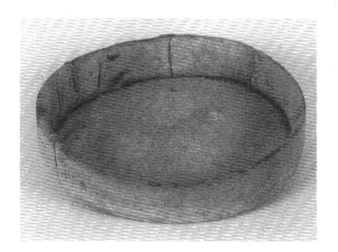

Looking at the first idea we find that in Ireland and indeed in other Celtic countries — Scotland, Wales the Isle of Man and parts of England — the sieve or winnow was well-known. It was called a **Wecht, Wicht** or **Dallan** and was in use up until the end of rural farming methods at the beginning of the 1930s approximately.

The wecht was made by stretching a sheepskin over a willow or ash branch split along it's length, bound in place by bark strips and padded out by wool or grass. The wet skin was tucked in under itself, or lapped, holding tightly in place once dry. This is a common practice in drum making. The wecht was held by this rim during use.

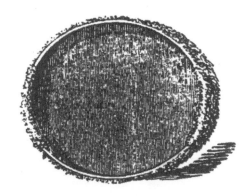

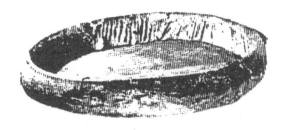

Séamus Tansey, a great Flute player from Gurteen, Co Sligo remembered that when he was younger the wecht was used to winnow grain and would be stored above the hearth. At evening time people would go to a certain céilidh house — usually an ordinary farmhouse nearby — where people would gather after a day's work in the fields to unwind while enjoying the music, storytelling and dancing. As the musicians struck up the wecht would be brought down from its place above the hearth and struck by hand in time with the music.

An Irish Farmyard c. 1905

As there were fewer agricultural workers because of mechanisation, music moved away from the rural areas and migrated towards the cities. Around this time the drum was made as a musical instrument with a thinner skin and sometimes old pennies or bottle tops for jingles.

Séan O'Riada suggested in the Radio Eireann broadcasts of 1962 that ; 'until fairly recently it was still used for its primary purpose - separating wheat from chaff. Hence, perhaps, its association with harvest festivals. In parts of Limerick and Clare it is still associated with, and played on, Hallowe'en.. . . it is also associated with. . . St.Stephens Day, when the wren boys parade, wearing straw costumes and playing flutes and Bodhráns.'. . .

The second idea suggests that as with many of the instruments used in Irish traditional music it came from elsewhere originally. This particular theory has many sub-theories as to exactly where and how they arrived on Erin's fair shore.

North Africa has many drums similar to the bodhrán; the Girbal (lit. sieve) for example, Morocco has the Bandir, Algeria the Duff and in China's Peking province the Shou Gu is played. Many of the above drums share common features some have jingles (as did many bodhráns in the 50s and 60s) and some have snares but all this seems to prove to me is that many cultures have evolved a similar drum.

Yacoub Addy (Ghana) with frame drum

Duff framedrums, Ethiopia

It has been suggested that established ancient trade routes brought these types of drums from North Africa through Spain and up to the south coast of Ireland or that the shamanistic tradition (from areas around Lapland for example) influenced the early Irish who came in contact with them.

The big problem with these theories is the lack of any physical evidence to back up any of these theories. It is possible that it was not considered significant by people in the past to record what may have been a common household utensil. The other difficulty is the simple fact that wood and skin can decay easily leaving little physical evidence for the anthropologists. So far in my research I can not find any convincing evidence to support any of the 'traveller' theories, if anyone has any archive material out there, drop me a line please!

Hassan Erraji with Bendir drum (Morocco)

Frame drum, Tunisia

Duff, Afghanistan

The most interesting part of the history for me is the rapid development of diverse styles over the last forty years. In the early 50s the great Séan O'Riada saw a production of the J.B.Keane play '**Sive**' in which an actor comes on playing the bodhrán. This is where, according to some people, Seán got his inspiration for including it in his musical group, '**Ceoltoirí Chualann**'. Some even suggest that he was a major influence in getting people to use a stick. Certainly his positive attitude was a great help.

Co.Limerick, 1946

Tony McMahon and Sean O Riada

Over the years players have been moving away from playing with the hand, using the stick styles of North Kerry (double end) and Limerick (which uses the small looped half stick) in an attempt to raise the art of Bodhrán playing. A recent development involves tying together end to end two of the brushes used by "pop" and Jazz drummers and playing double end style. Whatever next!

South Ghana framedrum

BIBLIOGRAPHY

McCrickard J. E. [n.d.] "The Bodhrán"
Pub. Fieldfare Arts and Design, Glastonbury
ISBN 1-870500 - 15 - 6

O Riada Séan [1982] "Our Musical Heritage"
Dolmen Press   .Portlaoise.
ISBN. 0-85105 - 389 - 0

O' Súlleabháin. Michael [1984] "The Bodhrán", Waltons   Dublin

O' Súlleabháin Michael [Mar/Apr 1974]
"Treoir" , Dublin

O' Súlleabháin Michael [1974] "Treoir", Vol.6.No.5 Dublin

Sutch David [1983]
"The Bodhrán, the Black Sheep of the Family"
Galpin Society Journal Vol XXXVIII, London

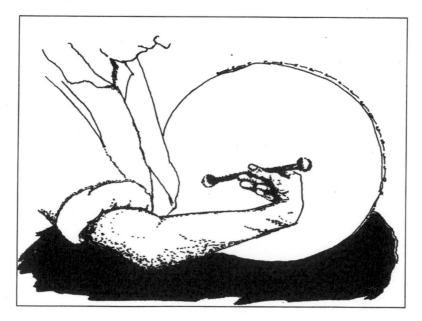

26. DISCOGRAPHY

Some recommended recordings featuring the Bodhrán. In each case the player's name is in brackets. Particularly good tracks are listed below.

Antonio Breschi "Mezulari"
Elkar S.A.   ELK 101
('Hopi' Hopkins)
Side 2 Track 1 1st Half
A thematic concept -type album with an exceptional bodhran part in this section.

Máirtín O'Connor "Perpetual Motion"
Claddagh   CCF26
(Colm Murphy)
Side 1 Tracks 1 & 3
Side 2 Tracks 4, 5 & 7
An unusual non - Trad Irish album requires tight, controlled playing .great stuff!

Boys of the Lough "The Pipers broken Finger"
Transatlantic Records   TRA33
(Robin Morton)
Side 1 Track 4
Side 2 Tracks 1, 6 & 7

Josie McDermott "Darby's Farewell"
Ossian   OSS 20
Topic   12TS325
(Robin Morton)
Traditional approach to playing.
Side 1 Tracks 6 & 9
Side 2 Tracks 2,7 & 8.

"The Coleman Co. Traditional Society"
Leader   LEA 2044
(Tommy Toolan & Seamus Donaghue)
Most tracks shared more or less equally. The style is very 1950's and the Bodhrán is called a Tambourine on the Record sleeve. a good example of early technique.

Paddy Taylor "Boy in the gap"
Claddagh   CC8
(Peadar Mercier)
Side 1 Tracks 3 & 8
Side 2 Tracks 3 & 8

Seamus Tansey "Seamus Tansey with Eddie Corcoran"
(Both alternate playing)
Leader   LEA2005
Most tracks feature a Bodhrán with jingles.

The Corries "Stovies"
Dara   DARA stereo P.A. 036
(Ronny Brown & Roy Williamson)
Side 1 Track 3 R.B.
Side 2 Track 3 R.W.
Scots Artistes of note who feature Bodhrán in their songs.

Altan   The Red Crow"
Green Linnet   CSIF 1109
(Ringo McDonagh,Donal Lunny,)
 Track 2 &4   , Track 7
A Brilliant band, fast hard driving donegal jigs and reels.

Mary Bergin "Feadoga Stain"
Gael Linn   CEF 071
(Ringo Mc Donagh)
Most tracks. A very good album with clear playing .A must
for your collection.

Sean Ryan "Take the air"
Gael Linn   CEF 142
(Ringo McDonagh)
Most tracks. As above.

Easy Club "Chance or Design"
Rel records   REL 479
(Jim Sutherland)
Side 1 Tracks 2 & 3
Side 2 Track 5   } With The stick.
Side 1 Tracks 1 & 3
Side 2 Track 5   } With The Brush.
You must Buy This Recording if You want to hear modern
playing of the highest order. S2 Tr 5 has a fantastic Bodhran
solo worth buying the recording for.

Stocktons Wing "Stocktons Wing"
Tara   TARA 2004   (Tommy Hayes)
Side 2   Track 5   .Most tracks feature this great player.
Another must featuring one of the top players around.

Donal Lunny "Donal Lunny"
Gael Linn   CEF 133 (Damien Quinn)
Most tracks. A perfect example of dynamic playing by a
talented
contemporary player. A good addition to your collection.

The Bothy Band were one of Ireland's top folk groups in the
70's
 and have made quite a few recordings. Donal Lunny's
playing is
almost understated and makes use of cross rhythms to
superb effect.

Bothy Band "Out of the wind into the sun"
Mulligan   Lun 013   (Donal Lunny)
Side 1 Tracks 3 & 5

Bothy Band
"Old Hag you have Killed me"
Polydor   2383417   (Donal Lunny)
Side 1 Tracks 1,4,& 7
Side 2 Track 6

Gary Shannon and Orflaith ní Bhriain
."Lose the Head"
      ?   BMM 1
(Mossie Griffin)
Most tracks, A great album with superb singing and playing.
Get it if you wish to hear the latest in top-class Bodhrán
technique.

The Chieftains have over the years made many recordings
which feature the Bodhrán .you could try the following as a
start:

The Chieftains"Chieftains 1"
Claddagh   CC2   (David Fallon)

The Chieftains"Chieftains 3"
Claddagh   CC10 (Peadar Mercier)

The Chieftains"Chieftains Live"
Claddagh   CC21   (Kevin Conneff)

Kevin Conneff "The week before Easter"
Claddagh   CCf23
(Kevin Conneff)
Bodhrán accompaniment to songs and Tunes.

De Dannan are yet another Irish traditional group who have
 influenced many others.Their Bodhrán player Johnny"Ringo"
 McDonagh is in great demand for recording sessions.

De Dannan "Ballroom"
WEA   DDLP1
("Ringo" Mc Donagh)
Most Tracks.

De Dannan "Best of De Dannan"
Shannachie   79047 ("Ringo" Mc Donagh)
Most Tracks.

Moving Hearts "Moving Hearts "
WEA   WEAK58387   (Christy Moore)
Most Tracks, but in the foreground in a more rock setting.

Davy Spillane "Atlantic Bridge"
Tara   TA3019
(Christy Moore)
Cooking Vinyl COOKoo9
More of the same contemporary integration, especially Side 1
Track 2.

Davy Spillane "Shadow Hunter"
Tara   TARA 3023
(Christy Moore)
Cooking Vinyl COOKo30
Listen to Side 1 Track 1 and Side 2   Tracks 1 & 2

Planxty made many beautifully evocative recordings utilising
traditional instruments in the 70's and 80's .you should try to
add a couple to your collection.

Planxty "Words and Music"
WEA   WEA24 0101 1
(Christy Moore)

Planxty "The woman I loved so well"
Tara   TARA 3005
(Christy Moore)

Steáfán Hannigan, ,"Natural Selection"
Ossian   OSS 58
Most tracks.

Apart from this book and the accompanying Demo-cassette,(Ossian OSS 57), Steáfán has also produced a solo tape — Natural Selection (Ossian, OSS 58) on which he may be heard playing pipes, whistles, bouzouki, flute and of course the bodhrán!

All the music on this tape forms the final section in this book, by way of a musical bonus. The music may be used for practically all melody-instruments.

Finally, a video with all the material discussed in this book is now also available (Ossian, OSV1), making this the most complete package of traditional music tuition ever shown.

Swallow's Tail

Gravel Walks To Granny

Star of Munster

Milltown Jig (or Boys of the Town)

Austin Barrett's

Coppers and Brass

Plains of Boyle

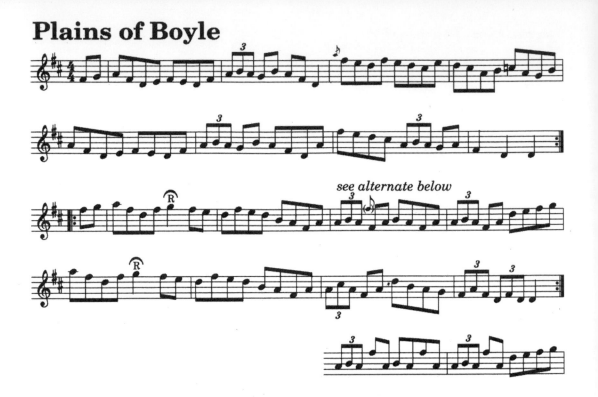

Sweep's Hornpipe or Belfast Hornpipe

Caliope House

The Ship In Full Sail

Ducks on the Pond

Kitchen Girl

Primrose Lass

Cat's Got the Measles (Keel Row)

Green Grow the Rushes Oh

Maid in the Cherry Tree

The Old Bush

The Milliner's Daughter

alternative

Phoenix Reel or Sharon Shannons

Ciaran Kelly's

The Mananán Reel or John Stenson's Reel

Tiocfaidh tú Abhaile Liom?
(Will You Come Home With Me?)

The Wheels of the World

Lark in the Morning

The Congress Reel

The Green Gates

see alternative below

alternative

Egar's Polka

Ballydesmond no 1

Slow Air Cailín na gruaige doinne

Freely

The Gold Ring (An Fáinne Óir)

The Butterfly

Laurel Tree

Ivy Leaf

Farewell To Erin

Ossian Publications produce and distribute a large range of traditional music in bookform and CD's. For an up-to-date list of all our productions please contact Music Sales Limited.

www.musicsales.com.

CD TRACK LISTING

	Section Title	Tune Name
1	INTRODUCTION	Lads of Laois (m)
2	PREPARING TO PLAY	—
3	DYNAMIC PLAYING	—
4	SKINSOUNDS	—
5	REELS 1	Congress Reel (s)
6	JIGS 1	Caliope House (s)
7	REELS 2	Ciaran Kelly's (m)
8	JIGS 2	Tiocfaidh Tú Abhaile Liom (s)
9	TRIPLETS	Ship in Full Sail (m)
10	RIM PLAYING	Laurel Tree (s)
11	REELS 3	Maid in the Cherry Tree
12	JIGS 3	Mananán Jig (m)
13	COMPLEX REELS	Laurel Tree, Ivy Leaf, Farewell to Ireland (s)
14	COMPLEX JIGS	Milltown Jig, Austin Barrett's, Coppers & Brass (s)
15	OTHER STYLES	Examples on Tambourine

	Section Title	Tune Name
16	HORNPIPES	Plains of Boyle (s)
17	SLIP JIGS	The (Admiral) Butterfly
18	MARCHES	The Pikeman's March (s)
19	POLKAS	Ballydesmond (s)
20	SLIDES	Dennis Murphy (s) &
	WALTZES	The South Wind (s) &
	MAZURKAS	La Ciapa Rusa (s)
21	TUNES TO PLAY	Primrose Lass, Keel Row,
	ALONG WITH	Green Grow the Rushes O (s)

(s) = played by Steáfán Hannigan, (m) = played by Mananán

> To remove your CD from the plastic sleeve,
> lift the small lip to break the perforations.
> Replace the disc after use for convenient storage.